HOW I LOST MONEY IN REAL ESTATE BEFORE IT WAS FASHIONABLE

A CAUTIONARY TALE

D0880142

JL COLLINS

Author of *The Simple Path to Wealth*

Foreword by Kristy Shen, Author of *Quit Like a Millionaire*

jlcollinsnh.com

Cover Design: Jess LaGreca
Interior Illustrations: Nikolett Meresz
Interior Design: Mary Jaracz

ISBN: 978-1-7377241-1-7 (eBook)
        978-1-7377241-2-4 (Paperback)
        978-1-7377241-3-1 (Hardcover)

First Edition
Printed in the United States of America

*D*EDICATION

To my daughter Jessica. Should she
ever choose to buy real estate, may she
do it with her eyes wide open.

TABLE OF CONTENTS

Acknowledgements

I am an avid reader. As such, I have read the acknowledgement pages of many books. I've always scoffed. Sure, I'd think to myself, some people might have done a bit to smooth the rough edges, but the real heavy lifting was done by the author who is now just being nice.

Then I wrote my first book, *The Simple Path to Wealth*, and learned what it really takes to go from manuscript to published book. This book is no different and I would especially like to thank the following people who helped make it happen.

PROJECT MANAGEMENT

In a rare stroke of brilliance, for this book I engaged a project manager. **MK Williams** came to my attention from several sources I highly respect.

"You need to work with MK!"

"What's an MK?"

She is smart, highly organized, and a pleasure to work with. And boy howdy but she knows how to self-publish a book. She is an author in her own right, having published multiple novels and her own series of books on self-publishing and book marketing. You can find her prolific catalog at 1mkwilliams.com

Could I have published this book without her? Probably.

Would doing so have given me still more gray hairs and been less fun? Absolutely!

COVER DESIGN

Since the moment I first saw the work of **Jess LaGreca**, it seemed a perfect fit for the feel and tone of this book. Since sharing it as a work in progress, her cover design has received rave reviews. My guess is you would have given it one too, had you been asked. So when I say this graphic designer and illustrator did a brilliant job, I do so without fear of contradiction.

Where such talent comes from, who knows? I can tell you Jess comes from the greater New York area. She has past book design experience at Penguin Random House and Simon & Schuster, and she acquired her MFA from the Savannah College of Art and Design (SCAD). Jess is currently freelancing full-time as a cover and interior layout designer — jesslagreca.com. She is based in Boulder, Colorado.

ILLUSTRATIONS

Nikolett Meresz has been drawing since she was a child and even won awards for her work back then. So, of course, she went on to study law. She never dreamed she could make money with her art.

But after finishing her studies, and coming to her senses, she let her life lead her back to drawing. Realizing she could get paid for her work helped.

She also sings and plays guitar and has performed in live shows with a couple of her rockabilly bands.

For now, drawing remains her passion but not a day goes by without her music. Could be, someday in the future, I'll be able to say, "You know that famous rockabilly star? She's the one who illustrated my second book!" behance.net/piquepack

INTERIOR DESIGN

Mary Jaracz joins the publishing team for a second adventure after working on *The Simple Path to Wealth*. Easily lured by a challenge, she's won awards for her book designs, along with work done for a European rock band, and for several baking recipes and sewing projects.

Fearing no challenge, Mary, her husband, and two sons are renovating their 1800s farmhouse in the Midwest.

PROOFREADERS

I'm a bit obsessive about typos and grammatical errors in the books I read, and I was committed to expunging them from this one. These are the people who found all my errors and made it happen:

- **Andrew L Green**
  Andrew's degree in journalism honed his writing skills and attention to detail. He lives in Seattle with his wife and son, and works for Amazon in business development. Thanks to the advice of JL Collins and others like him, he plans to reach FI in 2022/2023.

- **Bill Melcher**
  Organic and URL-free since 1968. Having long been financially independent, Bill now fixes and flips cars as a hobby.

- **Bill Thompson**
  A former IT manager, Bill discovered the FIRE movement in late 2014 and subsequently retired at the end of 2015 at 58. While attending the 2015 Chautauqua, he met JL Collins and has been a follower ever since while also considering him a friend. He is and always will

remain an Index fund convert. Why mess with easy and effective?

- **Chris Sells**
  Chris is a product manager at Google and putters with personal finance management as a hobby. He wishes *The Simple Path to Wealth* had been published much earlier and saved him a lot of money and heartache. <u>sellsbrothers.com</u>

- **Elliot Riis**
  Elliot, M.S. (Literature), jumped at the chance to proofread this new book. He says, "The hours blissfully melted away as I worked. Plus, it was a thrill to communicate with my financial hero and to assist in this small way."

- **Kelly C Paradis, PhD**
  Dr. Paradis is an Associate Professor of Medical Physics and Associate Chair of Equity and Wellness in the Department of Radiation Oncology at Michigan Medicine. She also proofread *The Simple Path to Wealth*. She loves science, discovery, and kitchen dance parties with her husband and two little girls.

- **Kyle Landis-Marinello**
  Kyle is the author of *Personal Finance and Investing*. He's a public interest environmental lawyer who dove into personal finance and learned how to improve his family's finances by $300,000 in one year. personalfinanceauthor.com

- **Richard Carey**
  Rich is a recently retired Air Force officer who also proofread *The Simple Path to Wealth*. He bought 30 rental units while stationed overseas. Now back in the US, he self-manages those properties and focuses on conservative real estate investing principles. richonmoney.com

FOREWORD

Kristy Shen (millennial-revolution.com) graciously agreed to write the foreword. She is a major force in the world of financial independence and has been a longtime supporter of my blog, previous book, and investing approach. She is the co-author of the best-selling book *Quit Like a Millionaire*. She has also been a speaker at my annual **Chautauqua** (fichautauqua.com) event in Europe since 2017. Those were reasons enough to ask her. The fact that she readily agreed and then proceeded to turn out the brilliant piece that follows, is humbling. I owe you, my friend.

EMOTIONAL SUPPORT

Creating this book has been a long and sometimes stressful process. The emotional rollercoaster had me at times depressed, at times foaming-at-the-mouth raving, and at times giddy with delight. My wife **Jane** endured it all without stabbing me in my sleep. That there is not an award for this is one of the great short-comings of our civilization.

In short, with all their help, this book is as good as I can make it. Any shortcomings, flaws, or inaccuracies are entirely mine and very likely result from those few moments when I failed to follow their wise counsel.

Thank you for reading it.

FOREWORD

Some of you are going to hate this book.

Specifically, the house pumpers, the unscrupulous real estate agents, and the legions of homeowners who endlessly blast panic-inducing messages at their kids like "you can't afford NOT to buy a house" or "rent is throwing your money away" and "killing yourself to climb aboard the real estate train before it leaves the station forever is the only financial strategy that will lead anywhere good."

You know people like this. You work with people like this. You're probably related to people like this.

And those people are going to hate this book.

Because this book reveals that those people are, to put it delicately, full of crap.

Real estate is not a slam-dunk investment. In fact, if anyone ever tells you *anything* is a slam-dunk investment, they are lying and, in all likelihood, trying to sell it to you.

That's why the world needs people like JL Collins.

JL and I first met in 2016. I had been so frustrated and bombarded by all this outdated "advice" that I recorded a 10-minute video ranting about it, which later became viral and, many years later, formed the basis of my book *Quit Like a Millionaire*. To my complete surprise, JL saw the video, emailed me, and told me it was spot on and he loved it. This, despite the fact that I had spent the entire video blasting his generation.

Right away, I knew we would become best friends.

Because JL Collins isn't your typical Boomer. In fact, he's the most anti-Boomer Boomer I know. Because JL Collins doesn't bullshit. He tells you the truth. And he does it so you can avoid stepping on all the real estate landmines.

Told with the same humor and honesty of his international best seller, *The Simple Path to Wealth*, this is the sobering, cautionary tale every generation needs as an antidote to the real estate madness. Or as JL puts it, to avoid an "alligator – a real estate investment that is eating you alive."

Best of all, it teaches you lessons you will never forget. If you think you know the math behind real estate, think again. The tax savings alone from learning how real-estate depreciation truly works will more than pay for this book.

You will learn invaluable lessons such as:

- Renting can be cheaper than owning.
- A loss can still be taxed by Uncle Sam, so make sure you understand cost basis.
- Condos are not necessarily less expensive to maintain than single-family houses.
- The property you bought for yourself is very unlikely to make financial sense as a rental.
- Landlords don't get to set the rent based on their costs and desired profit: Mr. Market does.

JL has learned all the hard lessons and made all the mistakes in real estate investing so you won't have to.

Housing is important. We all need to live somewhere. How we choose to house ourselves is one of the most important life decisions we will ever make. Don't make this life-altering decision without reading this book first. It could save you hundreds of thousands of dollars and give you years of your life back.

Plus, you can use it to smack those home pumpers across the face when they try to trick you into a "guaranteed investment."

—Kristy Shen, co-author of *Quit Like a Millionaire*

$\mathcal{I}$NTRODUCTION

Ever since I first wrote this story and posted it as a five-part series on my blog, I've thought it would make for an entertaining illustrated book.

It was a painful saga to live through. But now, decades later, I can finally see the humor and enjoy it for the instructive, engaging tale it is.

My hope is, reading this you will learn from my mistakes rather than making expensive ones of your own. And I hope it is clear these lessons apply to much more than just real estate.

As with my first book, other than the Foreword, Introduction, and Lessons Learned, there is nothing here you can't find and read for free on my blog. That is by design and intention. Neither this nor *The Simple Path to Wealth* would exist without the support and encouragement of my blog readers.

As before, the writing has been more polished, and I trust this story is more complete and compelling for the effort. You be the judge.

One major — and I think very successful — addition here not to be found on the blog are the illustrations. I can't draw stick figures myself, but **Nikolett Meresz** certainly can. I am proud and grateful to feature her work here.

This is a true story. Even the names and initials are the same because, well, why the hell not?

CHAPTER I

Impossibly Naïve

Nowadays, everybody has a tale of money lost in real estate. Of dreams and cash evaporated. It has become all the rage.

Hard perhaps to believe now, but time was, not so long ago, real estate was considered a "can't lose" proposition. People said things like, "Buy land. It can only go up. They're not making any more of it." "Houses can only go up in value. You can't lose." And other people didn't laugh at them. No, really. They laughed at me.

That's because, all through the 1980s, 1990s, and well into the 2000s, I was saying, "Oh yes, you can." And I had the sad tale to back it up.

In January 1979, I was happily renting in Chicago and had returned from a trip to visit my mother in Florida. Life was good. My career was going well. I was making some bucks. I was thinking about buying a Porsche.

No sooner had I walked in the door than my phone began to ring with an especially insistent tone. It was my pal and old college roommate, Steve.

"Where the hell have you been?" he said. "I've been trying to reach you all week."

These were the days before cell phones. Before answering machines, even.

A few months earlier, we'd had breakfast together in a local cafe. Steve had the idea that we should partner and buy a 2-flat, a Chicago term for a 2-family building with one apartment per floor. He'd take one apartment and I the other. Seemed like a good idea. Everybody was touting the soundness of investing in real estate and extolling the tax advantages. This included Steve's banker father who was willing to pave the way to financing for us. No small thing in those days of rampant inflation and high — 11.2% in 1979 — mortgage rates.

After eating, we walked across the street to a local real estate broker's office. We told the agent what we had in mind and that our budget was about $100,000 — a significant sum at the time (about $385,000 in 2021 dollars, in fact). He asked if we were willing and able to take on a rehab project. We said "no" on both counts. He said in that case, there was no possibility. We thanked him and left.

A couple of points at this juncture. What the hell was he thinking? Looking back, the market in that Chicago neighborhood in that price range should have been brimming with options. And what the hell were *we* thinking just taking one guy's word for it and letting it drop? A 2-flat would have been, in hindsight, a far sounder investment than the debacle to come.

Now personally I didn't much care. I was a few years out of school, my career humming along nicely. I was single, making good money, and enjoying the carefree life of a renter — although I didn't fully appreciate it at the time.

Steve, however, was motivated. That's why he called again. He'd kept looking. He had found his Shangri-La. He had just put money down on a condo and couldn't wait to tell me about it. He wanted to be sure I had a shot at one before they were all gone. Condos were red-hot in that cold Chicago winter. Everyone knew they could only go up in value. Prices were rising fast.

This one was in an elegant old 1920s-era 3-story courtyard building right on magnificent Lake Michigan. The developer was gutting the apartments. Each would have its own heating and AC systems. Everything would be new inside the units

while maintaining the stately vintage exterior — the ideal combination in my mind. I went to check it out.

I looked at a 1-bedroom on the top floor for $40,000. It didn't have a lake view. Those units were all gone, but the back stairs from this one led right down to the lakeside patio common area. It was an empty shell, demolished to the studs, broken plaster bits lying across the floors. A mess for sure, but I could see the potential, and the courtyard view wasn't bad either.

I took all the upgrades — which added another $5,000 to the price — wrote a check for the $5,000 deposit and signed the papers. The developer YP and I shook hands. There were smiles all around. It was February. My new home was scheduled to be completed on August 1st. My lease ended on September 30th, giving me a couple months' cushion for the unexpected. My, but I was clever in this planning. What could possibly go wrong?

Yes, I can hear you screaming at the page.

No, I didn't look at anything else. No, I didn't check out the developer. No, I didn't run any numbers. I figured Steve and his banker dad had done all that pesky legwork. Why cover old ground?

Yes, I was impossibly naïve.

Over the next several months, as I shared the good news with friends and colleagues, I received wise and consistent advice: Visit the worksite often. Monitor the progress. Stay on top of it. All this, of course, I failed to do. I didn't have time. I didn't have the expertise. I didn't have the inclination. They were the experts. I had effectively hired them to do a job, why would I want to get in the way? Why indeed.

Along about mid-August, having heard nothing, I decided to go have a look. Two weeks past the finish date, and two weeks until my planned move, only the final touches should have been remaining. I was eager to see my new home.

I was horrified. It was completely untouched. Not a speck of broken plaster had been disturbed. Not even a dust mote floated in the still air.

In a passion, I stormed down to YP's office. Moments later, fists on his desk, looming over his shrinking form, I inquired, perhaps not entirely politely, what the hell was going on? He assured me all was well. Two weeks was *plenty* of time. Moreover, if I was unhappy (*if??*), he would cheerfully refund my money. That calmed me a bit.

I sat back and thought for a moment. I knew it wasn't going to happen in two weeks, but my lease ran through September. That gave me, and them, an extra cushion of four weeks. YP seemed sincere. I wanted the apartment.

Then I made my second big mistake.

"No," I said. "I don't want the money back. I want the apartment. Just get it done." And I left.

Now, finally, I began to follow that earlier and excellent advice. Every few days I showed up. I encouraged. I bullied. I ranted. I praised — although finding reasons for this was vanishingly hard. More than once, YP again offered me my money back. More than once, I said no.

This dragged on for weeks.

I went to my landlords, three Croatian brothers I had been renting from for several years. They did a great job running the building, and I in turn was a great tenant. They were delighted to let me continue renting on a month-to-month basis. It pays to live quietly, deliver your rent reliably and early, and not trash the place.

Slowly, my apartment began to take shape. But each step forward meant another step back. Other condo owners in the building were discovering the same problems. They too, began to apply pressure. YP's work crew was woefully inexperienced and far too small to get it all done. But few of my

fellow owners were willing to be as demanding as I, and none were more intimidating to have scowling in his office. Progress was made, but not enough.

August turned to September, September to October. The leaves colored and fell. The wind off the lake turned chill. I reached the end of my patience. The apartment was about 80% done, but I was finished.

One day in his office I said, "YP, I'm going to accept your offer. I'll take my money back now."

"No," he said, "I can't do that."

Looking back, I realize now he meant literally: there was no way he could. He had no money left.

"Here in our contract," I said, "it clearly states if the apartment is not finished within six weeks of the original move-in date, I have the right to demand my deposit back. I am exercising that right."

"No," he said.

"You have to," I said. "It's in the contract."

"So sue me," he said.

The conversation went downhill from there.

A few days later, in Wayne's office, I was raving. Wayne was my big sister's lawyer, and I was in for an education.

CHAPTER II
The Limits of the Law

Here's what YP had been doing:

He had acquired the building with bank financing and gutted it. Maybe at this point he genuinely planned a real project or maybe it was a scam from the start. Hard to tell.

In any event, attractive literature had been prepared showing floor plans and glorious images of the finished units. He carved out a sales office on the first floor and within a month had sold all 58 apartments. They were due for completion and closing beginning in April and running through August. The market was red-hot.

Now, I'll never know if this was by design or incompetence, but when the first few units were due for delivery, they weren't ready. Buyers were incensed. They demanded their money back. YP cheerfully refunded it, and then he promptly resold the apartments for 15% more than before. Prices were rising that fast.

The bank was still happy, and he must have been thrilled. The cash (in the form of the down payments) was rolling in, and he didn't have to actually close on the places or do the work of finishing them. Instead, he simply resold them for more money.

Planned or not, this became his standard operating procedure. It's why he was so willing, eager even, to offer me my money back right into September. But what he didn't know then, what none of us did, was that the Chicago condo market was starting to tank, and fast. Just as he was refunding deposit after deposit to buyers smarter than I, it was all about to go off a cliff.

Suddenly these repossessed condos were no longer selling. Suddenly his fully sold-out building was half empty. Suddenly there were no more buyers.

The cash flow had dried up and the bank was getting very, very nervous. Now YP was faced with actually doing the work and finishing the building. And here I was saying, "OK, give me my money back." But by then, there was no money to give.

Suddenly he was forced to say, "No."

So, a few days later in Wayne's office, I was raving and I was in for a harsh lesson in legal realities.

"I want to sue this miserable, smug little bastard," I said.

Wayne said nothing.

"I want to crush him. I want to leave him penniless. I want to hound him to the ends of the earth."

Wayne said nothing.

"I want justice," I said.

Wayne waited and watched me slowly get a grip.

Wayne was now my lawyer and a couple of decades my senior. Considerably wiser. He listened patiently without comment. He waited until my venting was done and I settled back into my chair, and into my righteous indignation. He had his assistant bring me a nice cup of soothing tea.

Then he spoke.

"JL," he said, "you are my client and as such I will do whatever you tell me to do. However, before you decide, there are a couple of things I feel compelled to share with you.

"As justified as you think...," he caught my glare, "...as you clearly are, if this goes to court there are no guarantees. YP will present his case and we will present ours. Both will seem reasonable to the judge, and he's not going to spend much time on a $5,000 issue. In all likelihood, he'll simply decide to split the difference and award you $2,500.

"Now please understand, winning this award is not the same as collecting it. If this YP is as sleazy as you say, you'll never see a dime.

"Then, too, the ruling could go against us. You'd get nothing.

"Oh, and you should know my fee to take it down this uncertain path will be $2,500. Win or lose. So, if you win and collect, you'll have just enough to pay me. If not, well I'll still want my $2,500.

"As I said before, you are the client and if you so instruct me, I'll begin the suit. But I can't, in good conscience, recommend this course of action."

"I guess," I said, "there really is no justice in the law."

"Of course not," he said. "Whatever gave you that idea?"

Silly me.

Wayne advised me to keep pushing to get the apartment finished, and he wrote a nicely threatening legal letter to YP to encourage his cooperation.

YP's cooperation certainly improved, but our letter had little to do with it. He had payments due to the bank. With the flow of new deposits dried up, he now needed to close on these apartments to get the balance due. He desperately needed cash. He needed my remaining $40,000, and that led him to his first major mistake.

He agreed to let me move in before we had actually closed. Which, of course, I promptly did.

Think about that for a moment. I'm not paying on a mortgage since I don't yet own the condo. I'm not paying rent since I don't have a lease. But now I have possession. I was living there, and it wasn't costing me a single dime. Hmmm. This had suddenly become a situation with potential.

The power had shifted. The apartment by now was substantially done. There were a couple dozen minor things that needed finishing, but nothing that made it unlivable, or even uncomfortable. I produced a detailed checklist of remaining jobs to be finished.

We set a closing date.

The day before closing, I reviewed my list, crossed off the few things they'd gotten done, and canceled the closing.

YP was in a panic. His lawyer was in a tizzy. Wayne asked me why I'd canceled.

"As much as I would like to," I said, "we can't close. The work is not yet complete."

We set another closing date with the understanding it would be. More things on my list did get done. But more remained. I canceled again the day before closing.

Once again, YP panicked and lawyers groaned. Wayne asked me why I canceled the closing again. Wayne, now growing concerned, asked me why I'd canceled.

"Nobody wants to close more than me," I said, perhaps lacking a bit in sincerity, "but the work is not yet complete."

This went on for weeks as they couldn't ever quite seem to finish the list and be done with it. But slowly my apartment grew ever closer to perfection, and I continued living rent and mortgage free. My small, perhaps petty, bit of vindication didn't hurt either.

Now it's important to understand, I never refused to close. That would have been unreasonable and might have gotten me evicted. In fact, I agreed readily to every proposed closing date YP suggested. With, of course, the caveat that the items on my now infamous list be completed to my satisfaction. Each time, his crew would get a couple done and each time I'd cancel the closing because the list wasn't finished.

Even Wayne started to pester me.

"JL," he said, "you can't keep canceling these closings. The law says when the place is substantially finished, and clearly it is, you are required to close."

Can you guess what I told him? That's right.

"Let him sue me," I said.

Mine was the most complete and polished joint in the place by the time we signed the papers. But there was still more misery yet to come. I had made Major Mistake #3: I had signed the papers.

CHAPTER III
ＴＨＥ ＢＡＴＴＬＥ ＩＳ ＪＯＩＮＥＤ

This is the story of Major Mistake #3.

As you might imagine, I was feeling pretty smug at this point. It had been a hard and frustrating road, but now I celebrated my ultimate success in the completion of my apartment.

Things looked good and I was feeling the thrill of victory. But I had lost sight of the bigger picture. I had no idea how a condo actually operated or how expensive getting this one operational would prove to be.

Let's take a moment and review:

- Major Mistake #1 was buying with no due diligence.
- Major Mistake #2 was not accepting the refund when offered.
- Signing the papers and closing on the place was Major Mistake #3.

No going back now. I owned it. With all the rights, privileges and, ahem, obligations that entailed.

I should have walked away.

I should have never signed. I should have abandoned my five grand and chalked it up as lessons learned. I should have returned to my beloved rental. But no. I signed, and in the process signed on for still more grief.

So now I own this $45,000 condo and a $40,000 mortgage. Principal and interest came to about $370 per month. The condo fee added another $100, for a total of $470 per month. This fee would shortly double as we buyers struggled to finish the common areas of the building, bringing my total monthly tab to $570. The rent on my carefree apartment? $165.

Granted, my apartment had been smaller, and it certainly wasn't providing the hard-core education I was now enduring. But it met my needs and would have saved me $305 a month for the first 9 months over condo living and $405 for the 11 months afterwards—$7,200 extra in total. Real money in those days (and $24,451 **total** in 2021 dollars), not to mention the time and grief. Instead, I now owned a piece of The American Dream.

His turnover game done, YP was now relentlessly focused on trying to get the individual units finished. This was not just due to the pressure from me and my fellow owners. He needed the cash that now only closings could offer. His contractors wanted to be paid. His bank wanted its money. For everybody on team YP, that became priority #1.

In the push to get the apartments finished and closed, all work on the common areas ground to a halt. Those of us who had moved in were living in a construction zone. Naturally, we turned to pushing for this general work on the building to be done. And naturally, YP resisted doing it. He needed all his skimpy resources focused on finishing the individual units so they could close. There was zero benefit for him in turning his attention to the common areas.

The state of the transition of ownership further complicated things. Since we owners were still so few, the terms of the condo agreement meant we couldn't yet form an association and board to operate the place. That privilege — along with our monthly assessment fees — went to the developer, YP. He was desperate for cash and these fees promptly disappeared into his general funds. None went to the operation or betterment of the building. That, of course, was critically important to us.

As a young guy with a blossoming career, the last thing I wanted were the chores of homeownership. I'd had a belly full of those taking care of my parents' place while emphysema slowly killed my father. When he died and my mom moved to Florida…painting, patching, mowing, raking, shoveling, and the like blessedly became things of my past. I intended to keep them there. Hence, the appeal of the chore-free condo life.

That proved true. Not a mower, paintbrush, rake, or shovel did I touch during my entire condo-owning experience. Instead, I became part of a guerrilla movement. A freedom fighter on a legal battlefield.

We fought for fiscal accountability of our condo fees. For the completion of work to the common areas. For basic services. For control of the association. And, like many guerrillas, just for the sake of fighting in the end.

These battles were ceaseless and devoured countless hours. We held endless meetings and formed countless strategies. We were all young and clueless.

But with each condo closing our numbers grew. We were a tight-knit, battle-scarred little group by the end. The fight dragged on for months. I began to long for the simplicity of just mowing a lawn.

By the middle of 1980, the Chicago condo market had utterly collapsed. Like a nightmare game of musical chairs, YP's sell-refund-resell game had left him stranded. The once sold-out building was now a half-empty and half-finished fiscal disaster and legal war zone. A completely unappealing prospect for additional buyers, if there were any additional buyers to be had.

One fine autumn day, YP disappeared into the night. He left the bank holding its unpaid and unpayable notes. He left us with the unfinished building, unpaid contractors, empty units, and a looted association fund. Last we heard, he had fled to his home country. Rumors that he is bricked up behind a basement wall are, I believe, unfounded. Although this would be in keeping with a fine Chicago tradition.

The war was over. Our enemy had fled the field of battle. We were left battered and bloody, yet still standing. All that was left was the rebuilding, and the taste of ashes in our mouths.

Our hardy little band of owners promptly formed an association and elected our first condo board. As a first order of business, we opened a bank account and began directing the monthly dues into it. Second, we doubled those dues. This is how my $100 monthly assessment jumped to $200. There was much to be done and no way around raising the funds to do it.

In the summer of 1981, the bank finally gave up and held an auction for the remaining 29 (of 58) units. Condos similar to mine went for $20,000 to $24,000 depending on the condition and percent completed. After two years of strife, labor, and anger, all were finally sold and the building was on the

mend. The common areas were done and looking spiffy. Finally, I could reclaim my free time and enjoy my new home.

I just had to forget it was worth half of what I had paid and was now costing me twice the association fees I'd signed on for. Oh, and I was deeply underwater on my mortgage.

The financial hemorrhaging, of course, had just begun.

CHAPTER IV

I Become a Landlord

It is said some are born to greatness, some seek greatness, and some have greatness thrust upon them. So, too, with land-lording. And I was definitely in the thrust-upon group.

So now the battles have ended and the dust has begun to settle. I'm a home (well, condo) owner! Got my very own personal little slice of The American Dream and all the benefits that entails. In a nutshell: higher monthly costs and a depreciating asset. Whoopee.

My carefree, comfortable, $165 apartment is slowly becoming a distant and fond memory. In its place, my condo each month bleeds away $570: $370 in principal and interest and $200 in association dues. Plus, it's lost half its value. Sweet!

But our newly formed association is hard at work and it's shaping up to be a nice place to live. With what we've all been through together, these are neighbors who know and respect each other. A very nice community is forming…and I, of course, am planning to move.

It is the fall of 1981 and I'm engaged to be married come spring. We're going to need (OK, want) a bigger place and after months of searching and copious amounts of due diligence (I may be a bit slow but I *do* learn), I've just closed on my own 2-flat. One apartment is occupied with the most miserable tenants I'll have to endure in my short land-lording career, and the other needs major renovations. Exactly as expected.

I move into the one needing the work and begin knocking down walls and ceilings. Seems I've developed a fondness for living in construction sites.

This leaves the problem of what to do with the condo. I can't sell it. Or rather, I can, but only for the $20,000 to $24,000 they sold for at auction. Of course, then I'd have to come up with the $16,000 to $20,000 I'm underwater on the mortgage to be rid of it. But I don't have that kind of cake laying around to make the bank whole. I do have my honor (and other assets) to keep me from just walking away. I'm stuck.

I know! I'll rent it. I'll become a landlord. What could be easier? Well, eating ground glass for a start.

Now, investment real estate can be a very profitable venture, but trust me when I tell you backing into it like I did is not the path you want to take. Maybe someday I'll tell the tale of my 2-flat, a strategically planned, much happier, and more profitable story.

This is more the story of how *not* to do it.

Renting my condo turns out to be surprisingly easy. I pass the word around to my friends in the building, and before long a lovely young woman has signed the lease. She will prove to be a wonderful tenant, and she'll even find me my next — and also wonderful — tenant when she departs a couple of years later. Her rent is $375 per month - the market rate. This will remain the market rate for the full six years I own the joint. This is an important point. Landlords don't get to set the rent based on their costs and desired profit. Mr. Market sets the rent, and he doesn't care even a tiny little bit about your needs and desires.

Oops. Remember this number: $570? With only $375 in rent, I'm now hemorrhaging $195 — *$30 more than my old $165 rent* — each and every month for the privilege of owning what has morphed into investment real estate. This will continue for the full 48 months I rent the place, costing me a total of $9,360. Then it will get much, much worse. I will come to learn this is common enough to have a name. It is called an "alligator" — a real estate investment that is eating you alive.

But on to happier things first.

In January 1982, I get a major promotion at work. I'm made publisher of the magazine I work for — the second youngest to hold such a position in the company's history. The youngest ever? He is the current CEO.

This means a move to Cleveland, and that means I can now justify turning the finishing work on the 2-flat over to professionals. I've had the fun of demolition and have done just enough of the reconstruction to realize I don't like it and I'm not good at it.

Finally, and best of all, in June we get married. It is the most wonderful wedding there ever was or ever will be. The *Chicago Sun-Times* even carries a Page 3 picture of us leaving the church in our horse-drawn carriage. It is the wedding Charles and Diana aspired to, but on a smaller and more tasteful scale.

By fall, my 2-flat is finished. My pal Steve, now also married and renting out his own condo, moves into it and for a discounted rent manages the place for me. The other unit, now minus the miserable tenants, rents quickly and profitably...proving if you are going to do this real estate investing thing, it works better with planning.

My bride and I move to Cleveland and we rent a beautiful, 17th-floor condo overlooking Lake Erie and

the most stunning sunsets I've ever seen anywhere in the world. Ah, the blissful, carefree renting life again at last!

I am now both a tenant and a landlord — very likely the best of both worlds. I have four rental units: two condos (one in Florida which is a whole other story) and my 2-flat.

Between my job and my better real estate investments, the $195 monthly hemorrhaging is manageable. Still, it grates, and I am always looking to sell. But the condo market has only gotten worse. Want to know how bad? I can't even get a real estate agent to take the listing. Yes, you read that correctly.

If you know anything about real estate, you are likely re-reading that last line in disbelief. If you don't, let me explain just a bit.

Real estate agents live for listings. Get the listing and when the property sells, no matter who finds the buyer, no matter what else (if anything) you do, you get half the commission.

Of course, good agents work hard marketing the properties they list. But here's the important thing to understand: they don't have to. They could, and some do, take the listing, put it up on the MLS (Multiple Listing Service) and do NOTHING but

wait. They don't even have to show it. The agents hauling around the potential buyers do that.

But in those days in Chicago, for condos like mine, the market was so absolutely wretched not a single agent was willing to do even that. *There's* a tough market for you. Add to the mix my living in another city and, well, selling just wasn't likely any time soon.

The rays of sunshine in all this turn out to be my tenants. Each is clean, pleasant, takes care of the place, pays the rent on time, and causes me no problems. The first two even find me their replacements as they leave. I've never even had to advertise the place. But when the third moves on, I find out just how special that's been.

Unlike the others, my third tenant doesn't find me her replacement. Of course, she is under no obligation to do so.

So once again, I pass the word that the place is available. Nothing. I advertise. Nothing. My little unit is in a glutted rental market. Until now I had no idea how lucky I was to have my little parade of good and reliable tenants. But at least now I understand why the market rent had been stuck at $375 during this period of otherwise high inflation.

Remember when I told you things would get much worse? Well, here we are. The place is not only un-sellable — it is now apparently un-rentable. My $195 monthly bloodletting? Turns out, those were the good old days. Now it's $570 out the door every month. This will last for a brutal 16 tenant-free months before, finally, I get it sold. Let's see: 16 x $570 = $9,120. Add in the previous $9,360, and we have an operating loss of $18,480 on a $45,000 "investment." So that would give us an ROI of...

...ah hell, I don't want to know.

In that terribly depressing paragraph above, hopefully you noticed the little nugget of gold — I did, ultimately, get it sold. Let's turn next to that happy tale and the snake in its garden.

You knew there'd be more snakes, right?

CHAPTER V

Sold, and the Taxman Cometh

One of the few good things to come from all this was the bond and friendship we beleaguered owners developed.

My pal, whose name I have somehow shamefully managed to forget, was now the condo association president, and he generously kept an eye on my place for me as it sat empty. He knew I was desperately interested in selling. One happy day a woman approached him to ask if he knew of any units available for sale in the building.

"Well," he said, "this is a very desirable building and units rarely come on the market. But, as luck would have it, I do know one owner who might be persuaded to part with his." And he gave her my number.

I understand he was able to say this with a straight face. Bless you and your subtlety, my friend. I should have remembered your name.

When she called, my heart soared. I wasted no time in arranging a business trip to Chicago.

We met. I showed her the condo. She loved it. (It was, despite the bitter tale surrounding it, quite a nice place.) Turns out her boyfriend lived in the building, and they wanted to be closer together. Guess what? His unit and mine shared an adjoining wall. They could, if they so chose, break this wall and create a single grand space.

Not only was this the building she wanted, my condo was for her the most perfect one. If only she'd been stupid…my stars would have been fully aligned. She was not. She was, curse it all, a lawyer — and a smart one at that.

"How much do you," she said coolly, "want for the place?"

"Well," I said as nonchalantly as I could manage, "I hear condo prices have been flat these past few years. I paid $45,000 for it back in '79. I could let it go for that." And then celebrate uncontrollably till my eyes fell out.

"I'll give you $35,000," she said, not blinking. This is a beautiful moment when, in the course of negotiations, you get to a price that works for you and the

60

rest is just how much icing will be on the cake. The weight of years was finally lifting.

A bit of back and forth and we settled on $40,000 — not coincidentally, exactly what I owed the bank.

The deal went through without a hitch. It was the end of 1986. After eight long years I was free, and it only cost me $23,480 — a $5,000 loss on the sale and the $18,480 total of the monthly bloodlettings. So that would give us an ROI of...

...ah hell, I don't want to know.

Then too, the 20 months I lived in it also cost me $7,200 more than if I had just kept renting my $165 a month apartment.

Of course, I'd had some tax breaks along the way that softened all this a bit, but who's counting?

The IRS, as it turns out, was counting.

According to them, I had a $15,000 profit and I now owed a $3,000 (20% at the time) capital gains tax on it. Surprised? Well, maybe not if you're a real estate investing pro, but I was stunned.

For the rest of us, here's how this works.

As I mentioned, with all that cash bleeding away each month, I was desperate for some relief. Turns out, when you own investment real estate, the acceptable business model allows you to assume the building will wear out over time. This is called "depreciation," and it is considered an operating expense. As such, it is deductible in the eyes of the IRS. Further, back when I was doing this, there was an option called "accelerated depreciation," and this is exactly what it sounds like. You can choose to state that your building is wearing out at a faster rate and thereby take a larger deduction over fewer years. Of course, I grabbed this with both hands like the drowning man I was.

Now here's the thing. The IRS is nobody's fool. When you sell, they are going to want their cut. Your taxable capital gain (or loss) is not the difference between what you paid and the selling price. It is the difference between your "cost basis" and the selling price.

"But wait," I hear you say, "you sold at a loss, JL. You sold for $40,000 and you paid $45,000. There is no gain to tax." You are half right. There is no gain, but there is a $15,000 "profit" to tax. "Cost basis," you see, is an entirely different thing than what you paid for the place.

The problem is the depreciation I'd been taking must now be accounted for. It amounted to $20,000 over the years. This $20,000 reduced my cost basis from the $45,000 purchase price to an adjusted cost basis of $25,000. Since I sold for $40,000, voila! — a $15,000 taxable gain.

The taxman giveth and the taxman taketh away.

Here, finally, my sad tale ends. This is the final tally:

- $18,480 in operating losses
- $5,000 capital loss on the sale
- $3,000 capital gains tax

$26,480 down the tubes.

That, my friends, was *serious cash* back then (about $63,100 in 2021 dollars, in fact).

When I really want to depress myself, I calculate what $26,480 invested in an index fund tracking the S&P 500 starting September 1986 would be worth today. By September 2021, it would have grown to ~**$1,050,853** at the S&P 500's 11.09% annual return with dividends reinvested for those 35 years. (~$423,146 at an inflation adjusted 8.24% annual return.)*

I shoulda bought a Porsche.

---

* https://dqydj.com/sp-500-return-calculator/
* https://www.calculator.net/investment-calculator.html

$\mathcal{L}$ESSONS $\mathcal{L}$EARNED

My hope is, reading this you will learn from my mistakes rather than making expensive ones of your own. And I hope it is clear these lessons apply to much more than just real estate.

So, just what are the lessons to be learned from this sad tale of woe? Here are a few of my takeaways...

Chapter I: Impossibly Naïve

1. Be very wary of "can't lose" propositions.

2. Don't do something just because those around you are doing it. Even if they are your friends. Maybe especially if they are your friends. Your mama probably scolded you more than once in your wayward youth saying, "If all your friends jumped off a cliff, would you?!"

Well, of course you would have! You were just a dopey kid back then. Time to stop being a dopey kid.

3. Don't do something just because a banker, real estate agent, guru, or other "authority" tells you it's a good idea. By all means, seek wise and professional counsel. But look at that advice through a sharp and critical lens. You are the one who is going to be living with your choices.

4. If someone tells you something can't be done, don't accept it as gospel. They could be wrong or simply have their own agenda. Move on and ask others, then decide.

5. If you are happily renting, keep renting. It is almost always cheaper than owning. There are many reasons to own, and some are even good. But these have much more to do with lifestyle than any potential investment return.

6. Shop around. Whenever you are buying anything, it pays to look at a range of alternatives. The advice of others can be useful, but it might well

apply more to their situation than to yours. They could also be just flat wrong.

7. If you ever have construction work done, visit the site often. Even if you have no construction experience, check the progress and ask questions. Lots can go wrong with remodeling and building projects and, for most workers, yours is just another job. Nobody cares about the outcome more than you. If you can't do this, if you don't have the time or inclination, seriously consider not taking it on at all. As almost anyone who has been through a construction project will tell you, it is not for the faint of heart.

8. When things are going from bad to worse and someone offers you an escape, grab it with both hands!

9. Be a great tenant. Pay your rent early, treat the property (and your landlord) with care and respect, and don't disturb your neighbors. It is the right thing to do, and it has value to your landlord. That value pays off in lower and fewer rent increases, more attentive service to problems, and a great referral when you move on. It might even buy you more time in a pinch, as it did for me.

10. What's that, you say? Your landlord doesn't care about such things and treats all the tenants terribly? Well, time to move on. If you are the kind of tenant I just described, there are landlords who'd love to have you.

Chapter II: The Limits of the Law

1. As the chapter title suggests, there are limits to the law. By all means, "get it in writing" when putting together a deal. Just don't naïvely assume this protects you.

2. Having a contract is one thing. Enforcing it is something entirely different. Enforcing it is expensive, time consuming, and often unproductive.

3. This exchange from the story bears repeating:
   "I guess there really is no justice in the law."
   "Of course not. Whatever gave you that idea?"
   Whatever indeed.

4. Turning to lawyers should be your last resort. Far better to negotiate, argue, and cajole on your own until your ears bleed from hearing your own voice.

5. When you find a lawyer who is honest enough to tell you not to hire them, you've found a good lawyer.

6. If you stumble upon an advantage, as I did, don't be shy in using it.

Chapter III: The Battle is Joined

1. If you get the chance to walk away from a bad deal, even if it costs money, carefully and unemotionally consider taking it. Don't fall prey to the "sunk cost fallacy." Just because you spent $10 on a ticket to a bad movie, you wouldn't sit through it till the end, right? You would? Well, there's the sunk cost fallacy in action. Throwing good money after bad, as the saying goes. Example: Don't be afraid to walk away from $5,000 to avoid losing five times as much later.

2. Compare the cost of renting versus that of owning before you buy, not as a postmortem on a deal gone bad.

3. Condos are not a path to carefree living. Yes, someone else will shovel the snow and cut the grass and replace the roof. But you will either have to work with your fellow owners to get these things done, or just accept their judgment on the what, when, how, and how much of it all.

4. Condos are not necessarily less expensive to maintain than single-family houses. Both are relentlessly trying to return to dust and both require an endless flow of money to keep that process at bay. The only difference is, with a house, you have a bit more control as to the timing of maintenance and repair, and, if you choose, you can trade some of your time and labor for the cost of professional help. With a condo you pay your dues (and special assessments) and let others decide.

Chapter IV: I Become a Landlord

1. Don't back into being a landlord. The property you bought for yourself is very unlikely to make financial sense as a rental.

2. People who convert their home into a rental because they can't sell it — or are unwilling to accept the loss if they do — tend to wind up with an "alligator." That is not a pet. It is a creature that slowly eats you alive financially.

3. If you think you want to invest in real estate, take the time to learn about investing in real estate — and land-lording. There is money to be made, but this is a business and as such it requires certain knowledge and skills. You can learn these the hard way backing into owning a rental, like I did. Or you can learn first, buy strategically, manage it well and, you know, actually make money doing it. Here are some great places to start: biggerpockets.com, CoachCarson.com, richonmoney.com, affordanything.com

4. Many people seem to think a landlord simply totals up the costs of operating the property, adds in a fat profit and, voila, comes up with the rent. But others, like me, have learned the hard way when backing into operating a rental: it just ain't so. "Landlords don't get to set the rent based on their costs and desired profit. Mr. Market sets the

rent, and he doesn't care even a tiny little bit about your needs and desires."

5. Good tenants are gold. See point #9 in the Chapter I section above. Good tenants will save you more time, energy, money, and grief than you can possibly imagine just reading this. Care for yours well. Pure gold.

Chapter V: Sold, and the Taxman Cometh

1. It pays to have friends. Without my condo association president friend, I might still own this damn thing.

2. When it comes time to sell, sell. Don't worry about having to take a loss or feeling you need/ deserve a certain price or profit. Your needs and desires don't determine the sales price. Just like with setting the rent, Mr. Market decides what your property is worth.

3. People who promote owning and investing in real estate love to tout the tax advantages. There

can be some. But they are rarely as attractive as presented. Run the numbers based on your tax bracket and against the standard tax deduction.

4. Some of these tax deductions turn out to be tax deferrals. You can deduct depreciation today, but come tomorrow when you sell, your Uncle Sam will expect his cut.

5. Sometimes the "magic of real estate" is turning an actual loss into a taxable gain. See #4 above.

In conclusion...

So, what to make of all this? Should you avoid buying condos, or any property at all? Of course not. But realize that there are many considerations, pitfalls, and hazards potentially in your path. Once you are aware of this, you'll find them more easily identified and avoided. And this applies to more than just buying real estate.

You can learn from my mistakes or your own. I hope you choose to learn from mine and go forward with your eyes wide open.

AFTERWORD

Way back in the spring of 2013, I attended an awards banquet with a friend of mine. In the course of our conversation, we got to discussing whether her single, unmarried, childless son should buy a house. She felt it would be a good investment.

The next day I dashed off the post below as a tongue-in-cheek bit of fluff around this idea. It took maybe an hour from rough draft to final polish, the shortest time writing one for me, ever.

Little did I know it would go on to become the single most popular post on my blog, and it remains so to this day, eight years later.

It has garnered me the most hate — from those who love their houses — and the most love — from those who embrace renting.

From my perspective, both miss the mark.

This is no more an anti-house rant than the sad tale told before is. Both are "cautionary tales" making the point that buying real estate is a serious commitment and it is fraught with pitfalls and challenges. It is best done well informed and eyes wide open.

Done well, it can give you a comfortable place to live or a great investment. Done poorly, it can be an endless source of grief.

If this is anti-anything, it is anti-the-all-too-common real estate industry propaganda that buying a house is always necessary, always a good investment, and always better than renting. It's not.

Certainly, houses sometimes rise dramatically in value, but sometimes they don't. Sometimes their value crumbles to dust. For every Austin, Texas or San Jose, California, there is a Detroit, Michigan or Gary, Indiana.

Who knows, maybe by the time you read this, the story will be about the stunning resurgence of Detroit and Gary and the sad decline of Austin and San Jose.

Personally, I have owned houses most of my adult life and mostly they worked out just fine. They provided the lifestyle we wanted at the time and appreciated a bit in value. But they also required an endless stream of maintenance and, like most homeowners, we were seduced into expensive renovations. Renting was cheaper, simpler, and the money saved performed better in our index funds.

Think of houses as an expensive indulgence. Nothing wrong with this if that is what your heart wants and your resources can easily afford. Just don't confuse them with investments.

For your enjoyment, here is that now infamous post...

Why Your House is a Terrible Investment

Homeownership has been called The American Religion, so I know I'm treading on dangerous ground here. But before you get out the tar and feathers, let's do a little thought experiment together.

Imagine, over a cup of coffee or a glass of wine, we get to talking about investments. Then maybe one of us, let's say you, says:

"Hey, I've got an idea. We're always talking about good investments. What if we came up with the worst possible investment we can construct? What might that look like?"

Well, let's see now (pulling out our lined yellow pad), let's make a list. To be really terrible:

- It should be not just an initial, but if we do it right, a relentlessly ongoing drain on the cash reserves of the owner.
- It should be illiquid. We'll make it something that takes weeks, no — wait — even better, months of time and effort to buy or sell.
- It should be expensive to buy and sell. We'll add very high transaction costs. Let's say 5% commissions on the deal, coming and going.
- It should be complex to buy or sell. That way we can ladle on lots of extra fees and reports and documents we can charge for.
- It should generate low returns. Certainly no more than the inflation rate. Maybe a bit less.
- It should be leveraged! Oh, oh this one is great! This is how we'll get people to swallow those low returns! If the price goes up a little bit, leverage will magnify this and people will convince themselves it's actually a good investment! Nah, don't worry about it. Most will never even consider that leverage is also very high risk and could just as easily wipe them out.
- It should be mortgaged! Another beauty of leverage. We can charge interest on the loans. Yep, and with just a little more effort we should easily be able to persuade people

who buy this thing to borrow money against it more than once.

- It should be unproductive. While we're talking about interest, let's be sure this investment we are creating never pays any. No dividends either, of course.
- It should be immobile. If we can fix it to one geographical spot, we can be sure at any given time only a tiny group of potential buyers for it will exist. Sometimes and in some places, none at all!
- It should be subject to the fortunes of one country, one state, one city, one town...No! One neighborhood! Imagine if our investment could somehow tie its owner to the fate of one narrow location. The risk could be enormous! A plant closes. A street gang moves in. A government goes crazy with taxes. An environmental disaster happens nearby. We could have an investment that not only crushes its owner's net worth but does so even as they are losing their job and income!
- It should be something that locks its owner in one geographical area. That'll limit their options and keep 'em docile for their employers!
- It should be expensive. Ideally, we'll make it so expensive that it will represent a

disproportionate percentage of a person's net worth. Nothing like squeezing out diversification to increase risk!

- It should be expensive to own, too! Let's make sure this investment requires an endless parade of repairs and maintenance without which it will crumble into dust.

- It should be fragile and easily damaged by weather, fire, vandalism, and the like! Now we can add on expensive insurance to cover these risks. Making sure, of course, the bad things that are most likely to happen aren't actually covered. Don't worry, we'll bury that in the fine print or maybe just charge extra for it.

- It should increase stress, lead to more divorces, but then be impossible to divide.

- It should require only one motivated — desperate — seller to drive down the price for the whole neighborhood.

- It should be heavily taxed, too! Let's get the Feds in on this. If it should go up in value, we'll go ahead and tax that gain. If it goes down in value should we offer a balancing tax deduction on the loss like with other investments? Nah.

- It should be taxed even more! Let's not forget our state and local governments. Why wait till this investment is sold? Unlike other investments, let's tax it each and every year. Oh, and let's raise those taxes anytime it goes up in value. Lower them when it goes down? Don't be silly.

- It should be something you can never really own. Since we are going to give the government the power to tax this investment every year, "owning" it will be just like sharecropping. We'll let them work it, maintain it, pay all the costs associated with it and, as long as they pay their annual rent (oops, I mean taxes) we'll let 'em stay in it. Unless we decide we want it.

- For that, we'll make it subject to eminent domain. You know, in case we figure that instead of getting our rent (oops, I mean taxes) we'd rather just take it away from them.

Boy howdy! That's quite a list! Any investment that ugly would make my skin crawl. In fact, I'm not sure you could rightly call anything with those characteristics an investment at all.

Then, too, the challenge would be to get anybody to buy this turkey. But we can. In fact, I bet we can get them not only to buy but to believe doing so is the fulfillment of a dream — The American Dream! — a national birthright.

Oh. Wait. I'm sorry. This was supposed to be about houses.

So a few weeks back I was at an awards banquet and sitting at our table of ten was a woman I know. She began talking about how she was encouraging her young son to buy a house. You know. Stop throwing away money on rent and start building equity.

I suggested that, since her son was single, living alone, and without children maybe he didn't actually need a house. That if he didn't need one and since they are lousy investments (and here I gave her a few reasons why this is so), maybe he should consider some alternatives instead. Or at least run the numbers first.

This didn't sit well, and it was a short conversation. It ended when she said, "Well, he'd be better off buying a house than a clapped-out Camaro!"

Well, yeah. Maybe so. If this is the only alternative.

Adjusting the Numbers for Inflation

In the telling of this tale, I have used the actual dollar figures as they were at the time. Looking back some 40 years or so, these probably seem impossibly low.

If you are curious, here they are in order of appearance along with their inflation adjusted 2021 equivalents. dollartimes.com/inflation/

1979	2021
$100,000	$384,747
$40,000	$153,899
$5,000	$19,237
$2,500	$9,619
$45,000	$173,136
$370	$1,424
$100	$385
$470	$1,808
$570	$2,193
$165	$635
$305	$1,173
$405	$1,558

1980	2021
$7,200	$24,451

1981	2021
$20,000	$60,365
$24,000	$72,438
$16,000	$48,292
$375	$1,132
$195	$589

1985	2021
$9,360	$23,153
$9,120	$22,560
$18,480	$45,713

1986	2021
$35,000	$83,409
$23,480	$55,955
$15,000	$35,747
$3,000	$7,149
$26,480	$63,105

Praise for This Book

"In an age where the dangling promise of real estate has become an elaborate fairy tale, JL Collins is our Aesop with this delightful and sobering modern-day cautionary fable. Quickly read; impossible to forget."

—Malachi Ray Rempen, Filmmaker, cartoonist, game designer, and ruffian, keenbean.studio

"Thinking of buying a new house or investing in real estate? Take off your rose-colored glasses and read this tale of how quickly things can go wrong. People don't share their losses like they do their wins! JL Collins is one of the brave ones who does."

—Vicki Cook, Co-author of *Estate Planning 101*, womenwhomoney.com

"JL Collins' entertaining, quick but powerful read is an important reminder that real estate investing can produce crippling losses which can multiply when naïveté and poor market conditions combine. Be prepared for serious self-study prior to investing in real estate. This book will show you why."

—Scott Trench, CEO, BiggerPockets.com

"This long-awaited follow-up to *The Simple Path to Wealth* drops wisdom and knowledge bombs left and right. And, like *The Simple Path to Wealth*, you don't even notice you're learning because the book is so much fun to read."

—Kyle Landis-Marinello, Author of *Personal Finance and Investing*, personalfinanceauthor.com

"JL Collins is a masterful writer, storyteller, and financial educator. In this book, JL tells a cautionary tale about his personal experience with the real estate market. If you think that buying real estate is always a 'no-brainer' decision, this book will teach you to think again."

—Brian Feroldi, brianferoldi.com

"In this book, JL Collins lays out in gory detail all the mistakes he made investing in real estate so you can see the pitfalls to avoid before they happen to you! The amount of wisdom available in this short book is almost hard to believe. We would all do well to internalize Collins' invaluable life lessons!"

—Brad Barrett, Co-host and co-founder of the ChooseFI Podcast, choosefi.com

"JL Collins has done it again! First he showed us *The Simple Path to Wealth*, now he demonstrates the complicated path to losing it. This book provides a powerful counter narrative to the adage that real estate is always profitable. This should be required reading for every would-be house buyer, hacker, flipper, and landlord over-confidently counting their future fortunes."

—Doc G, Host of the Earn & Invest Podcast, earnandinvest.com

"A whimsical tale of debt and destruction...of what-not-to-do as an early investor, told in a light-hearted and jovial tone. Easy-to-read, sound investing advice, perfect for the young person in your life who would much sooner listen to anyone but you."

—Zeona McIntyre, Real estate investor, agent, and mentor, ZeonaMcIntyre.com

"JL Collins writes about losing money in real estate, and I've already profited by simply following his advice on what NOT to do. This is a compelling horror story of what you can and can't control in home ownership and land-lording."

—Doug Nordman, Co-author (with his daughter) of *Raising Your Money-Savvy Family For Next Generation Financial Independence*

"'Only fools rush in' ...and this book will serve as a thoughtful pause when venturing into real estate. JL Collins, with his humor and storytelling, gives practical tips and might save you from a 'no-brainer deal' that should have required a bit more brainpower before signing on the dotted line."

—Jillian Johnsrud, Writer, speaker, coach, jillianjohnsrud.com

"This book is such a fun, relatable follow-up to the iconic *The Simple Path to Wealth*. As someone who lost a considerable amount of hard-earned money to a CON-tractor during an ill-advised flip, this book helps me remember the value of simply remaining debt-free and investing in low-cost index funds."

—Rashad Muhammad, Wealth building educator, youtube.com/c/WealthBuildingEducator

"Often, the best financial choice is to rent and invest the substantial costs of home ownership according to the lessons of JL Collins' *The Simple Path to Wealth*. Seldom does everything go perfectly or even smoothly with home ownership. And sometimes things go terribly, horribly awry... as you will soon discover."

—Jeremy Jacobson, Early retiree, blogger, and repeat homeowner, GoCurryCracker.com

"JL Collins is a natural storyteller and hilarious raconteur. Despite his cautionary tale of real estate woe, I found myself laughing out loud and thoroughly enjoying what could otherwise be a dry topic. This is a fun and quick read, filled with wise nuggets and essential food for thought for anyone thinking about diving into home ownership."

—Travis Shakespeare, Executive Producer and Director, *Playing with FIRE: The Documentary*

"JL Collins does it again with a new book on why real estate might not be the dream you think it is. This is his personal story of buying a condo and losing money on it month after month. The tale is haunting and humorous and gives an honest and refreshing no-nonsense take on buying a home and investing in real estate."

—Anita Dhake, thepowerofthrift.com

"Instantly transporting you back in time, this illustrated tale comes to life as you journey vicariously through JL's nightmare adventures in real estate ownership. This book is bursting with humor and life lessons to boot. It is a must read for any investor, real estate or otherwise."

—Accidentally Retired, Former entrepreneur and CEO, accidentallyretired.com

"This is the kind of financial lesson that sticks to your ribs! JL Collins proves what most investors have to learn the hard way: the money we lose has as much of a story to tell as the money we make. Every chapter was a reminder that sometimes our mistakes are our greatest teacher."

—Julien and Kiersten Saunders, Authors and co-creators, richandregular.com

"Before you invest in anything, you should study the awful, gut-wrenching, and unsexy details of what could go wrong. In this little gem of a book, JL Collins shares painful stories from his experience owning real estate, giving a valuable, honest assessment of real risks you could face. More than that, he shares truths about the fallibility of human decision-making that we are all susceptible to."

—Chad Carson, Author of *Retire Early With Real Estate*, <u>CoachCarson.com</u>

"JL once again shows us why we shouldn't blindly trust the investing industry, why we should always question what society expects of us (the American Dream), and why we should keep our eyes wide open when it comes to investing. These lessons could save you hundreds of thousands of dollars!"

—Sebastien Aguilar, Founder, educator, and community builder, <u>FireBelgium.com</u>

"There is a rather common misconception that real estate is a sure-fire winner all the time. It's not. JL's tale of condo woe is a prime example of just how wrong it can go when you jump in blindly with both feet. This story should be required reading for everyone before they buy their first property."

—Mindy Jensen, Host of BiggerPockets Money and author of *First Time Home Buyer*

"JL went from being a happy renter to owning a condo that he couldn't rent or even sell. If reality TV had been around in the early 80s, this would have made for great entertainment! JL experienced the worst of worst-case scenarios. Read this and learn from his mistakes before you put your money down."

—Carl Jensen, 1500Days.com & MileHighFI.com

"For fans of FI, armchair investors, and anyone who appreciates a cautionary tale wrapped in humor and wit, JL Collins delivers knowledge, perspective and intrigue as only an experienced contrarian could. In an age of algorithmic biases, JL challenges our preconceived notions of the American Dream, and makes us better for it."

—Scott Rieckens, Author and Executive Producer of *Playing with FIRE: The Documentary*

"I absolutely loved this honest and refreshing take on why real estate may not be the best investment for everyone. JL Collins' cautionary but entertaining tale will have you laughing and learning at the same time. This should be required reading for anyone considering purchasing real estate."

—Jamila Souffrant, Founder and host of journeytolaunch.com

"In a world that has been persuaded that the only way to live is home ownership, JL Collins is brave enough to stand up and point out the pitfalls and the crazy hype that has created this phenomenon. This is the book I *wish* I had been given when I was younger. I will be buying this for every 20-year-old I know."

—Alan Donegan, Co-founder Rebel Business School and Queen's Award for Enterprise winner alandonegan.com

"If the best way to learn is from mistakes, it's far better to learn from others' mistakes when possible. JL Collins generously, humorously, and entertainingly shares his investment mistakes in this short easy read, packed with wisdom that transcends the topic of real estate. A great book for anyone wanting to use their money to create a better way of life!"

—Chris Mamula, Primary author of *Choose FI: Your Blueprint to Financial Independence*, caniretireyet.com

"JL is teaching the inconvenient truths about real estate investing and doing so in a highly entertaining fashion. Most of the literature on this subject panders to our desire for hitting the easy button. No, it's not easy money. No, leverage is not the key to riches. No, it's not always better than investing in the stock market."

—Rich Carey, Military retiree, real estate educator, and investor, richonmoney.com

"JL captures your attention and your imagination as he walks you through a real estate investing masterclass from the annals of his very life. The story is powerful and so are the lessons taught from it. You will find yourself both challenged and encouraged after reading this book."

—Talaat and Tai McNeely, Personal finance educators, HisandHerMoney.com

"The reality of investing in real estate is that -- like stocks, bonds, commodities, or crypto -- you can lose your shirt if you're naïve, uninformed, and indeliberate. JL Collins' story, and the lessons he draws out at the end, illustrate the importance of studying the field, thinking critically, developing contingency plans, and challenging your assumptions about the market."

—Paula Pant, Host of the Afford Anything Podcast, affordanything.com

"JL Collins is one of the smartest investors I know, yet he made a bad real estate investment that cost him over $63,000 in today's dollars. The lessons he learned from that investment are invaluable and thankfully he's shared them in his engaging and entertaining new book. Tens of thousands of dollars worth of investing lessons for the price of a book...what a bargain!"

—The Mad Fientist, Host of the Financial Independence Podcast, madfientist.com

"40 years after JL Collins' real estate lesson, I learned my own lesson the hard way. Do yourself a favor and read this book before you invest a single penny in real estate. This is the book I wish I'd read before I became a landlord!"

—Gwen Merz, FieryMillennials.com

"When you invest in the stock market and it goes down, you take a loss. When you invest in real estate and it goes down, it can take you down with it. Packed with insights, JL Collins' entertaining disaster story should be required reading to offset the easy-money real estate narrative touted all too often by all too many."

—Chris Rusin, Investor and creator at LifeOutsideTheMaze.com

For More From the Author, Visit

JLCOLLINSNH.COM

CPSIA information can be obtained
at www.ICGtesting.com
Printed in the USA
LVHW092024200122
708857LV00012B/1341